God Says,

"I AM"

52

Inspirational
Poems and Pieces

Gloria Shell Mitchell

EncourageMint
Books

Gardena, CA

God Says, "I AM"
52 Inspirational Poems and Pieces

Other books by Gloria Shell Mitchell include:
The Garbage Man's Daughter Series:
Letting Go of Shame
Letting Go of SECRETS
Letting Go of STRESS
Letting Go of SCARS
My Knotty Decision
Bliss and Blisters in Love and Marriage
Desire After Divorce
And
Famous Faces in Dark Places

ISBN: 978-1-7334588-0-1

Cover and design: Samuel Okike (Psalmyy on Fiverr.com)
Editor: gabriellarw on Fiverr.com
Presented by: EncourageMint Books
www.encouragemintbooks.com

Printed in the United States of America

Dedication

to

Lovers of poetry and prose

In loving memory of

My mama, Minnie Pelzer Shell

and

My sister, Minnie Elizabeth Shell Carr

God Says, **"I AM"**

52 Inspirational Poems and Pieces

Contents

1.

Worthy Goals

A body that's lean
Money that's green
A house that's pristine
Surroundings that are serene
A flexible schedule, not routine
Protection from the unforeseen
A loving companion who's not mean
A person to answer the phone, not a machine
Genuineness in others, not a smokescreen
Help when needed, to appear on the scene
Complete trust in the Lord to intervene
A heart that's clean
A mind that's keen
To believe in the Christ you have not seen…
Is this list long enough for you to understand what I mean?

2.

The Paradox

God allows us to be born
      so we can die
He allows us to be sick
      so He can heal us
He allows us to be weak
      so He can make us strong
He allows us to be poor
      so He can make us rich in faith
He allows us to be impatient
      so He can teach us patience
He allows us to be lost
      so He can seek and save us
He allows us to be dirty with sin
      so He can cleanse us with his blood
He allows us to be discouraged
      so He can encourage us
He allows us to know grief
      so He can comfort us
He allows us to fall
      so He can pick us up
He allows us to have problems
      so He can solve them
He allows us to think we are wise
      so He can teach us foolishness
He allows us to be proud
      so He can humble us
He allows us to be broken
      so He can put us together again.

God allows us to backslide
    so He can bring us to repentance
He allows us to experience conflict
    so He can give us his peace
He allows us to feel empty
    so He can fill us with his Spirit
He allows us to experience hunger
    so He can feed us his Word
He allows us to be imprisoned
    so He can free us by his power
He allows us to cry
    so He can wipe away our tears
He allows us to know fear
    so He can teach us to trust him
He allows us to feel lonely
    so He can manifest his presence
He allows us to be rejected by man
    so He can show us his acceptance
He allows us to be hated by the world
    so He can shower us with love
He allows us to go through valleys
    so He can show us mountains
He allows us to be attacked by enemies
    so He can give us victory
He allows us to suffer hard trials
    so He can teach us how to rejoice
God allows us to die
    so we can live with him, forever.

What shall we then say to these things?
If God be for us, who can be against us?
                                    (Romans 8:31)

3.

God Says, "I Am"

If you say, "I'm lonely, Lord,"

> He says, "I am **Jehovah-Shammah**, the God of presence. I will never leave you alone. I shall be with you until the end of the world."

If you say, "I'm hungry, Lord,"

> He says, "I can feed you like I feed the birds of the air. The cattle on a thousand hills are mine, and all of the beasts of the fields are mine. I am the **Bread of Life**, **Jehovah-Jireh**, your provider."

If you say, "I'm sad, Lord,"

> He says, "I am the **Bright Morning Star**, the **Light of the World**. Weeping may endure for a night, but joy comes in the morning. I can cheer you with my gift of unspeakable joy."

If you say, "I'm so sinful, Lord,"

> He says, "I can wash away all your sins with my blood. I am **Jehovah-Tsidkenu**, the God of righteousness."

If you say, "I'm stubborn, Lord,"

He says, "I am **Jehovah-Elohim**, the self-existent **Creator**. I made you. I know all about you. I also know what to do to make your will agree with my will."

If you say, "I'm confused, Lord,"

He says, "I am <u>not</u> the author of confusion, but I am **the Way, the Truth, and the Life**. I am able to help you see that I am **Alpha and Omega**, the first and the last, the beginning and the end. I am the true and living **God,** and besides me, there is no God."

If you say, "I'm helpless, Lord,"

He says, "I am **Jehovah-Nissi**, your conqueror. I will fight your battles and all you have to do is be still. My banner over you is love, for I am Love."

If you say, "I'm sick, Lord,"

He says, "I can heal you. I am **Jehovah-Rapha**, the God who heals you. My arm is not shortened that I cannot save; nor my ear deaf that I cannot hear. Call to me and I will answer you. I sent my word to heal all manner of sickness and disease."

If you say, "I'm tired, Lord,"

He says, "I can strengthen you. I am **El-Shaddai**, the almighty, all-sufficient God. My grace is sufficient for you. My power is perfected in your weakness. The joy of the Lord is your strength."

If you say, "I'm troubled, Lord,"
>He says, "I can help you. I am **Jehovah-Shalom,** the **Prince of Peace.** You must be anxious for nothing, for I am in control."

If you say, "I'm naked, Lord,"
>He says, "I am **El Roi**, the God who sees. I can clothe you like I clothe the lilies of the field. I make all things beautiful in its time. I give the rainbow its colors and clothe the beasts of the fields. Trust me to clothe you too."

If you say, "I'm lost, Lord,"
>He says, "I can lead you to safety. I am **Jehovah-Rohi,** the good shepherd. I care for my sheep. You are very important to me."

If you say, "I'm dying, Lord,"
>He says, "I am the **Resurrection and the Life.** I defeated death, hell and the   grave on Calvary's cross long ago. Your life is in my hands. Your will to live will sustain you."

If you say, "I'm afraid, Lord,"
>He says, "Trust me with all your heart; lean not unto your own understanding. The fear of the Lord is the beginning of wisdom. I have not

given you a spirit of fear; but of power, and of love and of a sound mind. Fear not, little flock. I am **your Rock and your Fortress and your Deliverer."**

If you say, "I'm homeless, Lord,"
God says, "All of the houses and land are mine. I can even shelter you from the storms of life in my Ark of Safety whose name is **JESUS.**

Whatever you need, I've got it. Remember, this world is not your home. You're just passing through on your way to be with me. I am **Adonai**, your master. Believe that I am **Jehovah**, your eternally great, **I Am**.

4.

Pastor, I Am Leaving You in Charge

(Scene: An elder brother, the head of the family, walks into the house, looks at all the people present and then calls his little brother, Pastor, to come forward. He hands Pastor a Bible and speaks to him in the presence of all family members.)

MONOLOGUE

Pastor,

First, let me tell you about your name.

> **P** stands for preach and be persistent in praying God 's Word.
>
> **A** stands for adhere to and admonish in accordance with God's will.
>
> **S** stands for study, see, speak, and serve as God's watchman.
>
> **T** stands for teach, train, testify, and try the spirits God's way.
>
> **O** stands for oversee others without overlooking anyone in God's world.
>
> **R** stands for relax and rely on your spirit man to respond to God's wisdom.

Now, our Father in heaven has asked me to return home for a while. I have decided to leave you in charge of the house while I am gone.

Since you have been faithful to me ever since you were adopted into this family, I have chosen you to be in charge of my house during my absence. **Pastor**, never forget, that it was I who called you, chose you, and appointed you to oversee your brothers and sisters. I am going away to spend some time with Father, but I will return on a day and at an hour that no one knows but Father alone.

I expect you to take good care of all the members of this household. You must feed the babies milk. Give bread and meat to those who are more mature. Be sure to take care of the weak ones, heal the sick, bandage the wounds of those who hurt, comfort those who mourn, bring back those who have wandered off, and search for lost family members. Pastor, listen carefully to my words because they are life to you.

When the children obey you, they obey me. When they disobey you, they disobey me. I want you to know that I will be watching everything you say and do, even though you cannot see me. Don't LORD it over my people or teach them to do anything contrary to the written instructions I leave in this book. You, your wife, and children plus all your brothers and sisters must learn what I have written here and never stop following my instructions even if I don't return for two thousand years or more.

I will bring my rewards with me for your faithfulness. If you mislead even one of these little ones I have placed in your care, it would be better for you if an anchor were tied around your neck and you were thrown into the deepest part of the sea. Woe unto you if you should cause one of these little ones to turn away from me. BEWARE! Let no one cause you to think that you are the head of the household and not me.

Each of our Father's children has received at least one gift that is to be exercised to help build my house and keep it holy. Every gift is to be used for the glory of God and to benefit the entire family. Part of your job as overseer is to help them to discover and develop the gifts that your Helper, the Holy Spirit, has given according to his will.

This is a big house with lots of family members. You are expected to do everything decently and in order. Each one of your brothers and sisters is responsible for doing the task that I have assigned. In this way you can take care of your wife and children, and still be able to oversee my house without wearing yourself out. You are human and not God. You must eat properly, get rest, and sleep, exercise, spend time being husband and father, and most of all, spend time in prayer and meditation so you will think and act just as I would in any given situation. Let this mind be in you that is also in me.

Pastor you must always remember that I am the head of this house. I am not a respecter of persons. I assure you that my Father and I love all of you equally. Consider it an honor to be chosen to serve as God's under-shepherd. The greatest among you must be the servant of all. Out of all the family members I could have chosen to leave in charge of the sheep in this pasture, I chose you. Remember, my sheep hear my voice, for I am the good shepherd, and they follow me; a stranger's voice they will not follow.

When the children question your authority, especially the ones who will be born into the family, show them my written instructions. Make sure they study my Word daily so they will know what I expect of them. Train them to be doers of my Word and not hearers only. As a matter of fact, I will still be with you all, even while I am gone. I will see you but you won't see me as I appear now. Whenever you call to me I will answer you. Whatever you need, I've got it. If you need wisdom, just ask and I will gladly give it to you. In all your getting, get understanding. You do realize that to whom much is given, much is required. Your position involves some suffering. But be of good cheer for I will fight against those who fight against you. You will not be defeated, for greater is he that is in you than he that is in the world. Just trust in Me with all your heart and lean not unto your own understanding. In all your ways acknowledge me and I will direct your path.

Those who love me will obey all that I have commanded in this book called the Bible. If they love me, they will love you. If they hate me, they will hate you too. The children who did not know what I expected of them but did something will get a light whipping when I return. But those who do know what I expect of them and don't do it will get a heavy whipping. One day those who have been obedient will hear me say, "Well done my good and faithful servant, you have been faithful in a few things so now I will make you ruler over many."

I, your elder brother, Jesus, our Father's only begotten son, declare unto you this day in the presence of all family members in the house that I call my church, Pastor, I am leaving you in charge.

5.

Great Men Live Forever

Noah, the only righteous man on earth before God sent
the great flood.
Noah built the ark.

Abraham, a man of great faith, journeyed to the
Promised Land at God's command.
Abraham was a friend of God.

Isaac, learned that the Lord will provide a wife and
give you double for your trouble.
Isaac doubly blessed his younger son Jacob.

Jacob, wrestled with an angel and vowed not to let go
until he got his blessing.
Jacob had twelve sons—the tribes of Israel.

Joseph, promoted from the pit to the palace, saved his
family in a miraculous way.
Joseph had the gift of interpreting dreams.

Moses, the baby who grew up in pharaoh's palace, led
the Hebrews for forty years.
Moses received the Ten Commandments.

Joshua, strong and courageous, claimed all the land
upon which his feet did tread.
Joshua fought the battle of Jericho.

Samuel, a child called by God, became a prophet,
priest, and judge with an obedient heart.
Samuel anointed Israel's first kings.

David, promoted from shepherd of sheep to king of
God's people Israel.
David was the apple of God's eye.
Solomon, the wisest man who ever lived, had 300
wives and 700 concubines.
Solomon built a splendid temple for God.
John the Baptist announced the coming of the
Messiah and baptized Jesus too.
John the Baptist boldly spoke truth to power.
Jesus Christ, who walked on water, commanded the
raging sea to be still,
Jesus, Lord of lords and King of kings,
Jesus, both 100% man and 100% God at the
same time,
Jesus, demons tremble at the mention of his name,
Jesus, born of a virgin mother, crucified and
died on a cross,
Jesus, buried in a borrowed tomb, sealed by a stone,
Jesus arose from the grave three days after
laying down his life
Jesus ascended into heaven while men watched,
Jesus lives in heaven and on earth in the hearts
of all who believe in him.

Whereas, all should know that this list mentions familiar
names of great men, but today I'm pleased to add another.

Dr. Billy G. Ingram, the God-fearing founder and
beloved pastor of Maranatha Community Church
in Los Angeles for 30 years, freelance writer,
author, actor, educator, poet, percussionist,
humanitarian, and philanthropist will live forever

in the hearts of millions around the world. This great man modeled and produced *The Legacy*, a recording that others may imitate but none can duplicate because God chose him for this divine assignment. He completed his earthly works with excellence on March 8, 2011.

6.

STRESSED???

Remember, you are not alone.
> So rest in the LORD and
> wait patiently on Him.

Enjoy every moment of today
> recognizing that each experience
> requires your best, not extra, effort.

Let go of your anxieties and
> let God fight against those
> annoying spirits that fight against you.

Accept the fact that change is constant.
> Life's ever-increasing challenges
> demand action – not alarm.

e**X**pect aggravations and temptations.
> Their purpose is to steal your joy
> and destroy your peace.

Exercise your faith in God to perfect
everything that concerns you. Ask and
expect Him to show you his power to
turn those unhealthy feelings into
extraordinary blessings.

Having done all you know to do,
just stand still and behold the
salvation of the LORD!

7.

Can You Imagine That?

I can just imagine
How Mary must have felt
When an angel said, "You'll have a son."
But with a man she had not slept.

I can just imagine
What Joseph must have thought
Before news of the virgin birth
To him an angel brought.

I can just imagine
How Elizabeth did rejoice,
When her baby leapt inside the womb
at the sound of Mary's voice.

Can you imagine that? Can you imagine that?
Can you imagine that? I say, can you imagine that?

I can just imagine
The discussion there must have been
Before settling for the stable
There was no room in the inn.

I can just imagine
How shepherds in the field
Reacted to the presence of angels
When the birth of Christ was to them revealed.

I can just imagine
The babe lying in a manger
When people came to worship him
And not one of them was a stranger.
Can you imagine that? Can you imagine that?
Can you imagine that? I say, can you imagine that?

I can just imagine
How old Simeon's soul was blessed
To behold the baby Jesus
Before he took his rest.

I can just imagine
The brightness of that star
As it led the wise men from the east
To Bethlehem afar.

I can just imagine
How King Herod received the news
When the wise men asked, "Where is the babe
Born King of the Jews?"

Can you imagine that? Can you imagine that?
Can you imagine that? I say, can you imagine that?

I can just imagine
The excitement in the house that night
When an angel of the Lord warned Joseph
Set out for Egypt in flight.

I can just imagine
To him God's Word was simple
For his parents found him at twelve years old
Teaching in the temple.

I can just imagine
John the Baptist seeing that dove
The day he baptized Jesus
And heard a voice from heaven above.
Can you imagine that? Can you imagine that?
Can you imagine that? I say, can you imagine that?

I can just imagine
The miracles they saw
As disciples walked with Jesus
And the crowds that he did draw.

I can just imagine
My Lord on Calvary
Suffering and dying
For the sins of everybody.

I can just imagine
That look on Mary's face
When to the tomb she went one morn
And he had left that place.

Can you imagine that? Can you imagine that?
Can you imagine that? I say, can you imagine that?

I can just imagine
A world full of people like me
Who know the Savior lives
And Jesus Christ is he.

If you can just imagine
What Christ means to me
Shout, "Praise the Lord!
We've won the victory!"

Ready? Praise the Lord, we've won the victory!
Again. Praise the Lord, we've won the victory!
Once more. Praise the Lord, we've won the victory! Amen.

8.

Face That Giant

Face that giant called jealousy,
He seeks to stop you from loving me.
That monster's growth will not stop
Until he's convinced that he's on top.

Look in the mirror and
Face that giant called low self-esteem.
He wants you to feel like you're nobody,
When you are of royal birth—a king or a queen.

Face that giant called liar, known as your accuser.
Face that giant commonly called an abuser.
He wants to destroy you physically, verbally,
        and sexually my friend.
Don't you think the time has come
For your emotional, mental, financial and
        social abuse to end?

Face the giants called adultery and fornication—
        you know the two.
They aim to trick you into settling for less than
        God's best for you.
Come on! Face your long-time creditors
        and even your debtors.
Face all those giants who whipped you real good
        in the past.
Stand tall before them and rejoice in being free at last.

Face that giant with an attitude of love.
Expect help from the LORD above.
Face all those giants my friend, but don't you dare
Make one step toward any giant without prayer.

While armed soldiers were watching and
        no doubt praying,
A little lad named David approached
        the giant Goliath, saying,
"You come against me with a dagger, spear and sword
But I come against you in the name of the LORD!"

Greater is He that is in you
Than he that is in the world, don't you see?
Now go face that giant.
Jesus has already given you the victory!

9.

When

When you cry with those who weep
And share the pain of those who suffer
When you give out of your need
To help a hurting child or homeless brother
When you welcome strangers into your home
And prepare hearty meals for growing boys and girls
When you sit alone beside a quiet telephone
Hoping to talk to distant family and friends
When you forgive all who hurt you
And confess your faults with sincere love inside
When you bask in today's showers of blessings
Knowing God's eraser removed all your past mistakes
When you have known sickness and discouragement
And those times that break the human heart
When it seems like nobody understands your needs
Remember your friend Jesus sees, he knows,
He loves you, he really cares, and
When you least expect it, that's when he blesses you!

10.

It's Good to Know You

Not because you are so caring
Not because you are so kind
Not because you are so giving
Not because of your great mind

But because you laugh with those who laugh
And weep with those who weep
Because your thoughtfulness is so extensive
And your understanding is so deep

You treat me just like family
You include me in your prayer
You open up your home and heart
You welcome me right there

We're all one big family
The Bible tells us that, you know
My brother and my sister, you share your love
Every day in every way, and wherever you go.

Others agree it's good to know you.
Your love is both genuine and divine.
Most of all I'm truly grateful
To know that you're a friend of mine.

11.

Please God, Bless America

America – a rainbow of people speaking
    different dialects
    Flaunting their culture and their religious sects
    Striving to gain respect and maintain   individuality
    In a melting pot or salad bowl, that demands
    conformity.

Mothers – pre-teens to senior citizens practicing
    sexual immorality
    Reproducing young, in a perverted
    monogamous society
    Waiting in lines for welfare, WIC vouchers,
    food stamps, and such
    Not even expecting biological fathers to help
    out much.

Entertainment – 'tis evil personified in the youth of
    this land
    Violence via television, giant screen, video
    games or gun in hand
    Drugs, alcohol, sex, pornography, smoking, and
    junk foods abound
    Killing them gently, creating a shortage of burial
    space in the ground.

Religion – freedom to worship God is what our
forefathers sought.
To preserve religious freedom—not abolish it—
they fought.
Exalted today are idol gods: celebrities, fame,
money, and fancy cars
While the gospel is confined to beautiful
buildings, behind bars.

Ignorance – teach the children reading, writing,
and arithmetic, too
In this land of opportunity filled with much
to see and do.
Yet, in spite of high school diplomas and
expensive college degrees
People still struggle to earn enough to meet
their basic needs.

Culture – as American as baseball, hamburgers,
and apple pie,
Are school dropouts, gangs, death row inmates
waiting to die,
Imported goods, outsourced services, and land
sales to foreign investors
In a self-centered, tech-savvy society where
racial hatred festers.

Amnesty – deploy troops, welcome refugees from
around the world.
Having problems in your homeland? For you,
our flag is unfurled.
America, the land that once proclaimed English
her native tongue,
Home of the free, where both slaves and slave
masters have sung...

"God bless America, my home, sweet home."

Please God, bless America! Restore my home,
sweet home.

12.

Fifteen Blessings to Culminate Your Year

1. May your memories of past trials **dissipate** with each new day
2. May your joy **exacerbate** the frustrations of your enemies
3. May your Christian witness **educate** others near and far
4. May your genuine love **permeate** society
5. May your confidence and courage **eradicate** all fears
6. May your strength **humiliate** your opponents
7. May your humility **instigate** others to examine their attitudes
8. May your peace **illuminate** your trust in God
9. May your God **vindicate** you when you're unjustly accused
10. May your hunger and thirst for truth and righteousness cause you to **salivate**
11. May your quest for understanding **motivate** you to seek God's face
12. May your experiences of His greatness and goodness **activate** your worship
13. May your knowledge of God **annihilate** unbelief
14. May your victories over circumstances lead you to **celebrate**
15. May your patient hope prompt you to **participate** in praising God now.

I wish you a Merry Christmas and a prosperous new year!

13.

Fifteen Blessings If You Don't Vacillate

1. May your worries evaporate
2. May your peace punctuate confusion
3. May your wisdom elevate you
4. May your faith exterminate obstacles
5. May your love accommodate everybody
6. May your wealth accelerate
7. May your thoughts isolate the positive
8. May your actions illustrate
9. May your prayers escalate
10. May your joy circulate
11. May your forgiveness alleviate strife
12. May your kindness duplicate that of Christ
13. May your self-control exasperate your enemies
14. May your expectations stimulate your good deeds
15. May your God emancipate you

Wishing you a happy and prosperous New Year!

14.

Your Baby Is Special

Your baby is special, surely you will agree.
Although for months you speculate and anticipate
How the new arrival will look and what it will be,
The moment you hold that tiny person in your arms,
You know that God made your baby just for your family.

Your baby is special, a uniquely-blended personality,
Bundled with a host of needs that demand attention:
Affection, food, clothing, and instructions in morality,
The bills, spills, thrills, developing skills,
	and match of wills
Indicate that parenting is an awesome responsibility.

Children are a gift from the Lord; they are a real blessing.
(Psalm 127:3)

15.

My Daughter, At Seventeen

So now you're seventeen...
But what does that really mean?
Well, the joy of sweet sixteen will continue
With lots of other good things on the menu:

- ✓ An increased pizza craze

- ✓ A more attractive gaze

- ✓ More fashionable dress

- ✓ Less childlike playfulness

- ✓ A distinguished walk

- ✓ More intelligent talk

- ✓ Enhanced curves about the hips

- ✓ Constant attention to the lips

- ✓ Intense interest in hairstyles and pretty nails

- ✓ An appreciation for debonair males

- ✓ More willingness to express what you feel

- ✓ The ability to prepare a wholesome meal

- ✓ Sheer happiness in being licensed to drive

- ✓ Increased self-confidence—a necessity to survive

- ✓ A better choice of friends, more association with peers

✓ Application of wisdom acquired over the years

✓ Ability to exercise sound judgment and common sense

✓ Ability to handle money wisely, both dollars and cents

At seventeen you legally have just one more year
To remain in protective custody of parents you hold dear.
So, during this year, allow yourself to grow without fear.
Trust God to provide your protection
And He will lead you in the right direction.
Maintain a good reputation.
Show love in everything you do.
Remember, God loves you and I love you too!

16.

A Marriage Made in Heaven

How kind and thoughtful you are,
And such a cute couple too,
Giving, loving, caring, sharing...
Yes, these comments refer to both of you.

Your marriage sure is special.
See how God is working things out
As you grow towards perfection
He's knitting your hearts together without a doubt.

What a privilege it must be
For God to choose you for a sample
Of his match-making ability in marriage
And put you on display as a godly example.

Keep your eyes on Jesus.
He's right there with you on sunny and dark days.
As your unity blesses me and others
Blessings flow back to you in many ways.

*Delight yourself in the LORD and He will give you
the desires of your heart.*

(Psalm 37:4)

17.

The Couple's Creed

ASK, don't accuse
BUILD, don't destroy
COMPROMISE, don't curse
DISCUSS, don't fuss
ENCOURAGE, don't discourage
FREE, don't fault
GROW, don't stifle
HELP, don't hurt
INCLUDE, don't exclude
JOKE, don't jeer
KISS, don't despise
LOVE, don't abuse
MOTIVATE, don't aggravate
NOTICE, don't ignore
OFFER, don't beg
PRAY, don't punish
QUIT, don't push
RESPECT, don't reject
STIMULATE, don't tolerate
TRUST, don't disgust
UNDERGIRD, don't trample
VINDICATE, don't condemn
WORK, don't oppress
EXPECT, don't demand

YIELD, don't fight
Have a **ZEAL** to keep, not break, your wedding vows.

Be **AVAILABLE** for and not **ABSENT**
from one another
Be **FRIENDS** and not **FOES.**

"Do not try to work together as equals with unbelievers,
for it cannot be done.
How can right and wrong be partners?
How can light and darkness live together?"
(2 Corinthians 6:14 GNB)

18.

Mother, I'm Okay Now

Mother, when I am sad,
thoughts of you make me glad.
When I struggle with problems
that never seem to end,
I hear your voice saying,
"Child, turn them over to Jesus,
Trust Him to solve them, He's your best friend."
How many nights you must have lost sleep
Wondering, "Where is my lost sheep?"
I know God wiped away your tears
When my behavior improved in later years.

I'm glad you never gave up on me,
Like so many disappointed mothers do.
They don't realize God is answering their prayers
When they see what their wayward child
        is going through.

You've got to tell people how my life was a mess.
Now in God's eyes, I am a success.
I've learned to trust in Jesus and to obey His word.
Believe me, Mother, it has been
        a difficult learning process.

You taught me God's word and prayed with me too.
I watched you to see if what you'd say
        was what you'd do.

You did your best with me,
　　but God did the rest.
He taught me to depend on Jesus,
　　and put my faith to the test.
Mother, I'm okay now.
I only have one regret.
It's that God is still purging, pruning,
and shaping me,
And you can't see the best in me yet.

Look at me, Mother, I'm okay now.
None of your tears, prayers,
　　or labor have been in vain.
I'm a new person, just as you hoped
　　I would become.
I am happy in Jesus,
　　for truly I have been born-again.

"Those who sow in tears will reap with songs of joy" (Psalm 126:5).

19.

Loving You

You're a nice young man
With a heart pure as gold
You love and are loved by others
Both young folks and old

Your years have been like a roller coaster
Loaded with valleys and peaks
I'm mighty glad you keep hanging on though
Because your soul the devil seeks.

You are a marvelous creation in the image of God
Made especially for His very own use
Although, sometimes it may seem
Like your life has been filled with abuse.

Trust in the Lord, lean not to your own understanding
Study your Bible, be more patient and less demanding
Pray day and night, always without ceasing
If you're sincere, your blessings will be increasing.

My God still answers prayer
Your broken heart and dreams He will heal
Cast all your cares upon Him
And His plan for your life He will reveal.

Remember, Jesus loves you
And I love you too
Start loving yourself
It's really not too hard to do.
Seek the Lord while he may be found
Just call upon His name
When at last He sets you free
You'll never be the same.

Seek your happiness in JESUS
He will give you the desires of your heart
In the name of JESUS I speak right now
I command all your hurts, fears, and pains DEPART!

In writing this message to you, I've done my part
Now is the time for you to make a NEW START!

20.

Go Down Martin

Go on Martin, way down in the deep south,
Tell the oppressors, to let my people go.

Go on Martin, you sit-in and march, and ride,
Till all those closed doors for you are open wide.

Go on Martin, go march in Washington,
Proclaim freedom, across the nation.

Go on Martin, accept the Nobel Peace Prize,
Go on promoting nonviolence 'til you die.

Go on Martin, rejoice in yonder sky,
You trusted Jesus, and on him we still rely.

Go on children, learn to treat everybody right,
love all your neighbors, and walk by faith, not sight.

21.

Chains Set Us Free

Listen you poor, puny, proud black child
Standing on street corners and living in poverty.
Listen you educated, sophisticated woman and man
Seeking prosperity in this American society.
Don't you know: Chains set us free?

Listen to this black sister's voice
People of color everywhere.
It's time you realized, our release from oppression
Came only through the power of prayer.

From Africa our strong-willed ancestors
Brought rhythm, song and dance.
Such gifts lifted wounded spirits
And despite heavy burdens, they sought to advance.

In bondage slaves cried out to God
Just like the Israelites did in Egypt long ago.
The heavier the chains, the more fervent the prayers
Till finally God commanded, "Let My people go!"
Don't you know: Chains set us free?

Slave ships delivered chained bodies
Of a people who were born free
Growing from belief in native religions
      to belief in Jesus

They obeyed the LORD who urged,
    "Come unto me."

"Repent black child, come back to me,"
Is Jesus, the Savior's cry,
"I am the Lord and I change not,
On me you can still rely.

"Call to me and I will answer you,
And set you free once more.
Trust me, wait patiently, and remember,
From bondage to freedom, I, Alone, Am the Door."

You must never forget black child: Chains set us free.

So if the Son sets you free, you will be free indeed.
                    (John 8:36)

22.

Reflections of a Septuagenarian

"Ma, why are you so glad to turn seventy?"

"Child, seventy years is what the good Lord promised,
        eighty if we're strong;
The Bible is true, even the part that says
        the years are full of trouble and sorrow;
Life is soon over, and we are gone.
        Then there's no more tomorrow.
Many tomorrows came and went
        before I reached this birthday.
My mother, father, brothers, and sisters are gone
        and yet I'm still here is what I say.
I've got a stack of obituaries for grownups,
        teens and babies, too
Most were younger than I am,
        so I'm delighted to be right here with you.
That means no person, bullet, accident,
        disaster, illness or disease
Nor any other dreadful happening
        succeeded in snuffing out my life.

Celebrating birthdays is a matter of survival,
        Each year I have a personal revival
I like to take time out, challenge others, share
to rejoice in each moment if they'll accept a dare.
You young folks can enjoy whatever you have today
Because people in my generation paved the way.

I survived segregation and Jim Crow laws
  and made sure I stayed out of jail
I helped Mama clean up white folks houses
  all day to earn a dollar
I learned firsthand why Marvin Gaye sang,
  "It Make Me Wanna Holler."
I went upstairs to the movie theatres
  through the side entrance for Colored only
I learned how to hold my urine
  without wetting my panties
Cause we couldn't use public restrooms
  unless our job was to clean them
I didn't slap anybody's face,
  cry, or hide in disgrace
Neither did I pull a trigger
  when called a black nigger
My black teachers told us what to expect
  and gave us hope
They said education was the way out of oppression,
  not getting high on dope.

I made a fire to cook after gathering wood
  all year round
I never knew if a snake might bite me
  as I picked up sticks off the ground
I survived the stench from outhouses
  and thank God never fell through that seat
I read by kerosene lamp and carried many cans
  of that stuff home for heat
I walked long dusty roads because
  no city bus drove down our street
I washed clothes on a scrub board
  and graduated to a wringer washer

I drew buckets of water from a well and much later
        learned to use an electric dishwasher
That's progress, my child. That's progress.

I escaped the Vietnam War because I was a female
But I witnessed the killings of our fathers, sons,
        uncles and brothers—black men
It's no coincidence that many black women
        never had a husband or children
Genocide, mass incarceration and such
        cut off their semen
Heroine destroyed many, as sleeping men stood
        on sidewalks like frozen trees
Crack cocaine and the AIDS epidemic spread like a
        wildfire throughout our community
I'm so glad that STD didn't appear when
        I was messing around
By that time I'd quit playing church
        and was firmly planted on solid ground.
Like so many women, my heart was broken
        during the sexual revolution
But the peace and hope I found in salvation
        made me happy with my solution.
Wake Up Everybody and teach the children
        Teddy Pendergrass sang
I learned that war is not the answer,
        but love is a wonderful thang.

So, I've entered a new era in my life
I look back and wonder why all the bickering,
        turmoil and strife

Everybody receives the same twenty-four hours
        each day brings
But the Lord determines how much we keep
        and how much he'll take away
The game of life is kind of like spending time
        in arcades
Choose wisely, play safe and pray that you, too,
        can have decades
I must confess, at times gang wars and race riots
        worked my nerves for sure
Advancements and promotions followed setbacks,
        and helped me to mature.

Child, you are listening to a grateful woman that has
        seen her children grow up,
A cancer survivor who chooses to bless rather
        than hate those who persecute me
I'm a happy septuagenarian who eats meat
        and does not condemn the vegetarian
I'm glad to be an American who respects
        both the African and Hungarian.
Life is a precious gift given by God alone
Some suffer for a season, suffer long, or suffer not
It is not man, but God who determines our lot
And whatever my lot he has taught me to say,
        God is good and in the end
He is the one who will vindicate me.

Child, stay humble so God can use you.
And when you turn seventy,
take time to reflect on all He has brought you through.

23.

If You Can Believe

If you can believe a STORK brings a baby
      into the world In spite of the mom's tummy
      looking like she swallowed a basketball

If you can believe an EASTER BUNNY
      delivers colored eggs in pretty baskets
      with lots of frills and sweets to eat

If you can believe a TOOTH FAIRY
      miraculously finds her way into your bedroom
      on the same night you lose a tooth

Then you can believe MARY HAD A LITTLE LAMB.

If you can believe SANTA CLAUS
      flies throughout the night with a sleigh full of toys
      for every child in the world, slides down
      a chimney that does not exist,
      and knows everything you do

If you can believe JACK'S BEANSTALK grew high
      enough overnight to reach the home
      of a giant in the sky

If you can believe the BOOGEYMAN,
    whom nobody has ever seen, will frighten
    naughty children enough to make them behave

Then you can believe MARY HAD A LITTLE LAMB.

If you can believe SUPERMAN is really a man of steel
    with x-ray vision and the ability
    to dress in a telephone booth

If you can believe POPEYE, a weakling,
    gains supernatural strength after he
    squeezes open and consumes a can of spinach

If you can believe MICKEY MOUSE
    is a friend to people, and women run to him
    instead of away from him

Then you can believe, MARY HAD A LITTLE LAMB.

If you can believe PINOCCHIO's nose grew longer
    every time he told a lie, and a puppet
    turned into a real live boy

If you can believe THREE LITTLE PIGS
    lived in houses they built for themselves
    of straw, sticks, and bricks

Then you can believe MARY HAD A LITTLE LAMB.

If you can believe DUMBO, a floppy-eared elephant,
    can fly

If you can believe SNOW WHITE resurrected
after being kissed by a prince

if you can believe a pumpkin
    turned into CINDERELLA's coach
Then you can believe MARY HAD A LITTLE LAMB.

Mary did have a little lamb, and JESUS was his name.
His fleece was white as snow, for JESUS was without sin.
And everywhere that Mary went, the lamb was sure to go.
BELIEVE IN JESUS, THE LAMB OF GOD,
And with you He will surely go.

24.

As Sure As

As sure as water is wet,
     holes appear in a net
As sure as fire is hot,
     a rope gets tied in a knot
As sure as grass is green,
     pictures are made to be seen.
As sure as Jesus lives,
     all confessed sins he forgives.

As sure as jails have cells,
     the wedding symbol is bells
As sure as schools have teachers,
     churches have preachers
As sure as hospitals house the sick,
     a candle contains a wick
As sure as God is in heaven,
     His perfect number is seven.

As sure as sugar is sweet,
     people like to eat
As sure as ice is cold,
     young people do grow old
As sure as grapes grow on a vine,
     a freeway exit has a sign
As sure as the Bible is true,
     God made everything, plus me and you.

As sure as salt seasons meat,
        shoes are designed for two feet
As sure as roses are nice to smell,
        sick people long to get well
As sure as students will learn,
        trees in a forest fire will burn.
As sure as wind is air in motion,
        God alone controls the ocean.

As sure as a clock displays the time,
        disobeying God is a crime
As sure as healthy trees bear good fruit,
        everybody has a birthday suit
As sure as death is certain to come,
        one who rejects the truth is dumb
As sure as the sky contains the moon,
        Jesus is coming back very soon.

25.

A Minister's Lament

When sickness attacks a body, healing words I speak
When burdens get heavy, how to lighten the load I teach
When tiredness creeps in, seeking residence in my body,
I brush it off by focusing on the gospel that I preach.

Who am I that God would set me before His sheep?
My voice sounds the alarm for those who sleep.
When I try to say "No" to the one who bids me "Go!"
My ordered steps show that His commands I keep.

Though pressed by the masses to help them survive
I trust my inner witness to be my guide.
My passion to rescue the lost is surpassed by none
But God, our Maker, in whom I abide.

In times of despair when godly answers I seek
I hide in His bosom and let Him point the way
Around the arrows, pitfalls and snares the enemy brings.
I rest in Him and admire the beauty of each new day.

As I walk in the light speaking words of life
People push and tug, squeezing the life out of me.
Though I lead them to the Rock that is higher than I,
They still struggle with trusting a God they cannot see.

Help me, O Lord, as I minister your truth. Renew my mind
And speak so your voice can be plainly heard.
Godly wisdom I seek amid sweet communion with you
So I can feed the multitude what I glean from your Word.

26.

He's My Son

I cuddled my baby until he took his first few steps
And began to exercise his new freedom of choice,
I heard him babble words like "ma ma" and "da da"
Years before he developed a man's voice.

I lengthened the cord when he desired to run free
And monitored his activities and friendships, too
I trusted wisdom and instruction to guide him
Even in situations that were brand new.

I cheered when he participated in sporting events
Both at practice and games, like proud parents do.
I encouraged him through disappointments and losses
And his joyful response was, "Mom, I love you."

I listened to him no matter where or what he said
And embraced him when he was sick or sad
I shared my life stories to motivate and inspire
When I let go of the reins, he was glad and I got mad.

I cried at his high school graduation
And waved farewell when he joined the military.
I beamed when he clicked his heels and saluted.
What a handsome man in uniform he turned out to be.

I sent care packages from time to time
Just to ensure that he was eating right.
I asked my Lord to protect my child,
Each day when I prayed and each night.

I stockpiled memories before he went away
And rejoiced at hearing news of the battles won.
I pacified all my concerns with hope
And longed for his work on the battlefield to be done.

I know that a child is a precious gift from God.
He knows I did my best with the son placed in my care.
God gave him to me and war took him away, but
He's still my son. There's so much more I could share.

27.

An Unskilled Teacher's Lament

What are you doing to me
Oh, Lord? I pray
Don't you see the mentally challenged students
Who enter my classroom each day?

What causes these children
So dear to my heart
To buck like Broncos
Before the bell to start?

Some of their minds
Have gone on vacation to Mars,
While countless numbers of them
Howl and bark at the stars.

My Lord, I want to help
Bring them back to reality
But what a challenge
To get them to realize their real identity!

"It's all your fault we can't learn math,"
They yell and they scream
My lesson plans are a waste of time on teens
For whom education is merely a teacher's dream.

How do you overcome resistance to discipline the mind
And get them to face their own problems? I ask
To encourage them to change behavior,
For this unskilled teacher, is a daunting task.

28.

Sometimes

Sometimes we feel all alone
  With no one to comfort us
Sometimes we think no one cares
  About the troubles we endure
Sometimes we wish we could
  Steal away and find a safe place
Sometimes we reach out
  And it seems like no one responds
Sometimes we hope for joy
  And find nothing but sorrow
Sometimes we shed tears
  And wish for someone to dry our eyes
Sometimes we long for change
  Yet seem to get the same ole thing
Sometimes we pray and wait
  For answers that never seem to come
Sometimes, yes sometimes…
Sometimes we forget that we have a Father
  Who sees all things, knows all things,
  Is in control of all things and
  Promises never to leave us alone.

My friend, because this is one of those times
  When you need to know that someone cares,
  Someone loves you, someone is praying with
  you and for you, and understands the

heaviness of your heart,
I say to you my dear hurting friend,
"This pain shall pass."

Remember, weeping may endure for a night,
    But joy comes in the morning.

*Every test that you have experienced is the kind
that normally comes to people. But God keeps his promise
and will not allow you to be tested beyond your power to remain firm;
at the time you are put to the test, he will give you the strength to
endure it, and so provide you
with a way out.*

                    (1 Corinthians 10:13 TEV)

29.

It's Payday

I sprang out of bed, took a quick shower
And grabbed coffee and doughnuts in my haste
I arrived at work eight o'clock on the dot
And had not a moment to waste.

All day long I obeyed supervisor's orders to do this
And do that with barely a moment to rest
I completed all assignments and felt proud about it
Despite the rush, I'd done my best.

When at the pay window I stood fatigued
Expecting to receive my wage
I heard, "Man, no check for you today."
And I flew into a rage.

"I worked hard for my money!"
I yelled at the top of my voice.
"That you did, and pay you shall get," God replied.
"But money isn't your choice.

The wages of sin is death
Which this day you shall see
While you concentrated on pleasing men
You should have been pleasing me."

Final conclusion:
Fear God and obey his commands, for this is the duty of every person.
(Ecclesiastes 12:13)

30.

Heaven Is Our Goal

Teach us how short our life is,
so that we may become wise.

Sometimes we need to be reminded that
Heaven is our goal.
Heaven is not far from us—out there in
the great beyond, light years away;
But it's as close as the wink of an eye,
Just one blink
The flick of a finger
A fleeting glance
One breath
A single heartbeat
One moment in time
A tick without the tock
And voila! We'll be there.
In the twinkling of an eye
We will pass from earth to heaven.
Our loved ones can't come back to us,
but we can go to them.
But each of us must be ready.

Teach us how short our life is,
so that we may become wise.
                              (Psalm 90:12 GNB)

31.

Before Modesty Died

Teachers of truth are given less honor today,
but the effect of their teaching is often behind the scenes
impacting future generations.

Once upon a time America was called a Christian nation,
land of the free (as some people were) and home of the
brave. That was before so many of our young men were
killed in Vietnam, the Persian Gulf, Afghanistan, Kuwait,
Iraq, and on city streets.
Yes, that was during an era before modesty died.

Before modesty died, law-abiding American boys who didn't
run off to Canada registered for the draft and answered the
Marines' call for a few good men. It was a time when long
lines of registered voters stood at the polls because they
understood that people died for the privilege to vote.
Women fought for equal rights, knowing it was up to them
to make a change. If women don't fight for women's rights,
then who will?
Government of the people, by the people and for the people
works when every person gets involved in the political process.

Before modesty died, there was shame associated
with receiving a dishonorable discharge,
pride and respect for men in uniform,
and disappointment when rejected by the

all-volunteer Army.
Of course, all this was before modesty died.

Before modesty died, children were seen and not heard.
They dared not butt in on adult conversations, ask questions
or talk back. Any grown-up who saw a child doing wrong
would say, "Stop that!" and the child simply obeyed.

Before modesty died, nobody knew if a boy was wearing
boxers or jockey shorts because the boy's buns were neatly
packaged inside the correct size pants that were held up by a
leather belt.

Before modesty died, boys feared meeting a girl's father,
but built up the courage to go to her house anyway to get
acquainted with the entire family before courting
commenced.

Before modesty died, teachers could identify boys and girls
on their roster simply by their masculine or feminine names.
It was during a time when boys were proud to bear daddy's
name with a junior on the end and they mimicked daddy's
control in the household. Those were the days when men
proudly distributed cigars to announce the birth of a
newborn child.
Of course that was before modesty died and people started
using the terms deadbeat dad, and baby daddy and baby
mama drama became commonplace.

Before modesty died, a girl dared not be seen
showing the crack in her behind or crease in her bosom.
Some females even put tape on their nipples

to make them invisible. Those were called private parts and she knew good and well that she needed to preserve the sight of those areas for the man who would put a ring on her finger at the church house or courthouse.

Before modesty died, the fatty tissue protruding from a woman's top was securely tucked inside her brassiere, lest she provoke the ire of an elder woman who would hand her a shirt to cover up cleavage. Of course that's before modesty died and bras became an inconvenience that hindered the jiggles and pop outs. Oh, and panties—no longer a necessity—have been replaced by the thong so everything can just hang out. For some, wearing undergarments is no longer in vogue, even in fitting rooms when trying on new clothes.

Before modesty died, pregnant mothers wore maternity clothes so nobody would see their big, tight tummy, and all would know they were in a family way. It was back in the day when women wore slips to shield some stuff, and dress lengths were long enough to conceal other things, especially when she stooped down rather than leaned over to pick up a dime. Ahhh, that was during those days when pregnancy out of wedlock was embarrassing, and the thought of having an illegitimate child led to shotgun weddings.

Before modesty died, a person's sexual preference stayed in the closet and was nobody's business but their own. Back then two grown men didn't walk down the street holding hands unless one was blind or physically disabled. Who would have imagined seeing two women locked in a passionate kiss on the sidewalk in broad daylight, hordes of gay rights activists conducting parades in public streets, or news reports of a man having a baby when clearly everybody knows he doesn't have a womb? Before modesty died, men dared not wear pink shirts or pink ties merely to avoid false perceptions by others.

But all that was before modesty died. Modesty is dead now, so anything goes.

Before modesty died, people respected God's house
and went outside to smoke a cigarette or a joint.
It was back in the day when men had a little black book
and a lady waited for a man to call her because she
didn't want to appear too anxious and acquire the infamous
nickname, "Ho." She was told to keep her dress down and
pants up and be seen and not heard. Of course that was
before modesty died and modern day temple prostitution
became apparent on the church grounds and in the foyer.

Before modesty died, women waited to be noticed. Later on,
men started complaining about being pinched on the butt
and being offered an abundance of free milk without having
to own a cow or make any commitment whatsoever. Many
of these are the same men who used to insist that a woman
walk on his right side so he could protect her from potential
harm such as water that splashed from a passing car. Men
once opened doors for women rather than slam them in a
woman's face. Since modesty is dead, men and women
have no problem shopping at church like they're in a meat
market. Of course this is nothing new, but it was more
subtle back in the day before modesty died.

Before modesty died, there was no slurping or burping
at the dinner table, and the words, "excuse me" rolled off
the tongue all day long. Those words were spoken in the day

before home-cooked meals were replaced with greasy fast food and microwave dishes. There was a time when people actually talked to each other, pushed the chair beneath the table when they got up to leave so nobody would trip over chair legs, and basically considered other people more than themselves. That was back in the day when people got up and walked over to the television set to change the channel or adjust the antennae. You know, it was before you heard of a "couch potato" pushing buttons while fat accumulates around the midsection.

Before modesty died, a real live person showed up for a date and the libido was aroused by a natural physical attraction between a male and a female. Now, of course, that's as old-fashioned as when a man used to work two or three jobs to provide for his family while the wife stayed at home—however humble—and cared for the children. And then, along came the outbreak of the pornography epidemic and social media. Wow! Who could have imagined that a digitally enhanced individual on a cold inanimate object such as a computer screen would ever replace a warm body snuggled next to you?

Before modesty died, children knew not to sass any adult or say certain four-letter words in front of them unless they wanted to be slapped across the room. Before modesty died, just one look from a grown up checked a child's bad behavior or attitude. Of course that's before children began staring back and asking, "What are you looking at me like that for?" with no shame in their game. Once upon a time certain expletives—those profane words too foul for sensitive ears—were bleeped off the air. But not any more. From the crib children are trained to use the same power-packing punch lines as their adult role models in the home, on radio, television and computer.

Before modesty died, a child was embarrassed to earn an "F" on a report card. That was before the letter "F" took on the meaning of "fine" or "fabulous" rather than "FAIL." Fabulous underachievers have helped America rank as a finalist in failing schools. Yes, even famous star-studded California is a finalist. Hooray!

Before modesty died, parents showed up at PTA meetings and held schools and teachers accountable. Parents actually read teacher comments and responded by pulling the television plug. They either helped their child or children do homework or made sure it was done.

Before modesty died, people knew their neighbors by name, in fact they knew their neighborhood and worked to protect it. To a hurting neighbor, others came to the rescue to babysit, bring a dish, sit in silence, clean house, offer a few dollars or rally around a cause. Of course, that was before modesty died and people began keeping their personal business a secret until the divorce is made public, a foreclosure sign gets posted, or an incident makes the local or national news. Ouch! The death of modesty has destroyed many lives.

Before modesty died, she left a rich legacy of each one teach one, each one love one another, each one reach one with the love of Jesus Christ. Can you believe that many people balk at receiving their inheritance? Surely, you are not one of them, are you?

The modesty that died is expressed through your work ethic, motivation for self-improvement and tolerance of others who look different from you. Modesty is exhibited by humility, obedience, and simplicity rather than boastfulness, pride, a sense of entitlement, disregard for the wellbeing of others and living above your means.

Before modesty died, there was moderate behavior due to lessons at home on good manners. Every child once learned the words "thank you" and was quick to say it. Their outward appearance tended to avoid impropriety or indecency even when the spirit of rebellion was suppressed behind a façade. Ahh, but that was before modesty died.

Now, if you **cannot** relate to life before modesty died, then this is a history lesson for you. If you **can** relate, then this is a eulogy for modesty. But all hope for reform is not lost. Let's repent for neglecting our duty to get involved in civic affairs and allowing America to continue its downward spiral. It's never too late to stand up and speak out for what's right. You can begin right in your own home and in your own community.

Before modesty died, God gave us specific instructions. He already knew that we humans would tend to ignore our earthly teachers, and say and do as we please rather than what He wants us to do. So He gave us this friendly reminder for all of our days:

"Therefore, to him who knows to do good and does not do it, to him it is sin."

James 4:17 NKJV

32.

My Mom Is Gone

Those arms that held me close to her bosom
And cradled my helpless tiny frame
Those hands that changed my soiled pants
And prepared meals for me time and again

Those eyes that pierced the depths of my soul
And scooped out truths I tried in vain to conceal;
Those lips that guarded her soft voice,
And instructed, corrected and consoled with zeal;

Those feet that once chased after me
And allowed her to walk here and there,
Those ears so quick to listen
And to hear unspoken thoughts that showed her care;

Those body parts move no more for me.
For I peered down into an empty shell—
A cold facsimile of what used to be
A warm and loving, life-giving well.

Those days with Mom—
forever etched in my memory—
And cherished by a grateful heart
Were mere sprinkles of God's love for me,
The same God,
whose only begotten Son, Jesus, died on Calvary
Now assures me that with Him
my Mom is gone to spend eternity.

33.

A Tribute to Every Woman

Look around you girls, boys, men and women,
Take a good look at everything on earth
Do you realize that not a single human would exist
Had a girl or woman not chosen to give birth?

That's right, I said chosen to give birth.
Thank you mother that you did not abort
that life in your womb. It does not matter if
conception came through rape, incest, abuse, or consensual
sex. It happened. And now billions of people are testaments
of God's creative genius and your willingness to suffer for
the sake your child.
Mother, we love you for being strong and courageous.

You women who have not yet birthed a child,
But loved, nurtured and cared for foster, adopted,
abandoned, and orphaned sons and daughters
You women who embraced another woman's offspring
Because the mother was away in the military, ill,
incarcerated, incapacitated, Intoxicated,
or ignorant about what to do, and you women who look
after your neighbor's child or children,
You older women who sow into the life of
young mothers by word and by deed as certified
or unofficial teachers and trainers
Mother, we love you for being strong and courageous.

Nursing mothers, you show others the purpose for the
Natural milk jugs that some women take for granted when
they have them, and others pine or purchase accessories
when they don't have them.
Be encouraged you women who have had the myomectomy
and/or hysterectomy, your contribution to society is not
diminished by fibroids or sterility.
You matter. You do make a difference.
Mother figure or Godmother, we love you for being strong
and courageous.

If you delivered that bundle of joy while chained to a bed,
in the car on the way to the hospital, in a bathroom or secret
place, and abandoned your gift to the world on a doorstep,
in a trashcan or in a deserted place that God alone
understands,
Mother, we love you for being strong and courageous.

You women who once had a son or daughter that has
passed from this world to the next, you are still a mother.
You will never forget the child who once relied on you even
though your child self-destructed or fell victim to illness,
accident or foul play. You show us how to persevere in the
midst of despair and disappointment.
Mother, we love you for being strong and courageous.

You women with missing children, whether from abduction,
addiction, runaway, or missing in action after going off to
war, don't despair. Let the discovery of every missing child
that is reunited with family encourage you to remain hopeful.
Mother, we love you for being strong and courageous.

Women of every nation, tribe and tongue,
the burden of populating the earth rests with you.
Each individual has a divine assignment, so let no one
devalue you for what you do or don't do in terms of
preserving the human race. Both you and your contributions
to society are precious gifts from a loving God.
Mother, we love you for being strong and courageous.

Every woman would do well to heed this command spoken
by God: "**This is my command —be strong and
courageous! Do not be afraid or discouraged. For the
Lord your God is with you wherever you go.**"

(Joshua 1:9 NLT)

34.

Compassionate Elder Care

Family and friends call, visit, and send cards

Readers, storytellers and good listeners spend time in their presence

Able-bodied assistants offer strong arms, watchful eyes, and helping hands

Grateful nations praise them for their contributions to society

Inquisitive youngsters find them a rich storehouse of wisdom

Loving caregivers treat them with dignity and respect

Everyone knows that silver-haired elders reveal our destiny

*** Elders are FRAGILE ***
**Handle these gems with the same care you
want to receive.**

35.

Cry of the Barren Womb

*There are three things that are never satisfied, four that never say
'enough!': the grave, the barren womb, land which is never satisfied with
water, and fire, which never says, 'Enough!'*

(Proverbs 30:15b-16 NIV)

The womb or uterus, on which all births rely,
Is expected to be fruitful and multiply,
But when impacted by time, chance, and circumstance,
A womb that bears no fruit may ask, "Why?"

It matters not if the owner is rich or poor, bold or shy
Nor how often she will pray and cry,
or the couple will try.
Only the Most High God, who shows no partiality, knows
who will procreate, and why some wombs,
no babe will occupy.

Oh, what disappointment
when hope of giving birth does die
And the woman with the barren womb believes the lie
That God's favor rests on those who can conceive,
And for a man's affection,
with a fruitful woman she must vie.

Abram's mistress Hagar, gave birth
and cast a haughty eye.

She despised his barren wife, who could only sigh.
God intervened and reminded Sarai of her self-worth,
when neither a loving husband nor a surrogate's child
could satisfy.

A woman is not content with love, beauty,
and gifts that money can buy,
When she desires that unique bonding experience
no loving mother can deny.
Her womb yearns to shield and yield the miracle of life,
And failure to fulfill its purpose
makes the barren womb cry.

36.

My Baby's Room Is Empty

The movers came to clean out my house,
And said to one another
"Let's remove ALL the furniture!
The baby carriage and accessories
have served their purpose.
That old stuff is nothing but clutter now.
Don't let the mother see us
take everything out.
She might want to save her heirlooms:
uterus, cervix, tubes and ovaries.
They really must go,
and it's better to move them all at once.
Let's make it quick.
We've got other cleaning jobs today, too."

My baby's room is empty.
The movers sealed off the space and left.
Where did my baby furniture go?
Was it handled with utmost care?
Will it be reused or recycled?
As owner for decades,
why did I believe their "better out than in"
prevention strategy and problem-solving remedy?
Who decided that I could live
without furniture anyway?
Will that area of my house shrink

for lack of occupancy?
Will the vacuum bring ecstasy, grief or pain?
Will the plumbing to my bathroom expand?
Hist er rec to me!
Does anyone understand why the head of my house
grapples with questions at hand?

*And those members of the body which we think to be less honorable,
on these we bestow greater honor; and our unpresentable parts have
greater modesty.*

(1 Corinthians 12:23 NKJV)

37.

My Best Friend

My best friend is AVAILABLE,
he never slumbers or sleeps
He hears me whenever I call,
and his eyes upon me he keeps.

My best friend is BOLD,
sometimes his holy boldness overwhelms me
I find myself saying and doing daring things,
 uniquely orchestrated for my self-discovery.

My best friend is CARING,
I can leave all my worries with him
When I tell him my problems,
I know he takes care of them.

My best friend is DEPENDABLE,
he challenges me to put him to the test
And watch him shower me with good things,
so that I may be richly blessed.

My best friend is DISCIPLINED,
I wish I could be like that
He tells me to focus on my goals,
so I won't swallow a camel and strain a gnat.

My best friend is EXPERIENCED,
there's nothing he does not know
He sees everything, can do all things,
and there's no place he does not go.

My best friend is FAITHFUL,
with him no one can compare
I trust him for everything—
food, shelter and even clothes to wear.

My best friend is FORGIVING,
of every sincere person who asks him to
He even forgives his enemies, saying,
"They know not what they do."

My best friend is GENEROUS,
giving wisdom to all who ask
Whatever the need, he will provide aid
to accomplish the task.

My best friend is GENTLE,
he has a supernatural touch.
He corrects me when I do wrong,
His punishment is never too much.

My best friend is GOOD,
as sweet as honey from a bee
O taste and see that he is good,
 for he never changes on me.

My best friend is HONEST,
he's transparent whether I like it or not
His life is an open book,
and I read him a lot.

My best friend is HOSPITABLE,
right now he's preparing a place for me
In his father's house,
where one day with him I shall spend eternity.

My best friend is HUMBLE,
yes indeed, he will stoop to wash my dirty feet
He tells me to do the same for others,
not only family, but strangers I meet.

My best friend is IDEAL,
He'll never betray me or support racial or gender bias
As raindrops fall where they may,
he lights the path for the wicked and the pious.

My best friend is JOYFUL,
he declares weeping may endure for a night
But joy comes in the morning,
as long as I strive to live right.

My best friend is KIND,
a real compassionate friend
He strengthens and protects me,
and all my heartaches he will mend.

My best friend is LOVING,
he loves me unconditionally
I really love him a lot,
because he first loved me.

My best friend is LOYAL,
I can count on him don't you see?
Mother and father may abandon me,
but he will take care of me.

My best friend is MIGHTY,
day after day he does great and marvelous things
From healing the sick to giving hope to the hopeless,
I delight in the joy he brings.

My best friend is NOTABLE,
he's worthy of praise and honor from everyone on earth
Before my mother conceived me,
he knew my purpose and destiny, and timed my birth.

My best friend is OBEDIENT,
he always does his father's will.
If you're looking for a model child,
that role he can certainly fill.

My best friend is PATIENT,
I must W-A-I-T on his timing to become like this.
I wait on him to renew my strength,
for his blessings I dare not miss.

My best friend is PEACEFUL,
his peace surpasses all human understanding.
Happy are those who work for peace,
all peacemakers are in good standing.

My best friend is POWERFUL,
he defeats my strongest foe
With authority he speaks through me,
and commands my oppressors to "Go!"

My best friend is PUNCTUAL,
he never shows up late
Though sometimes he seems slow in coming,
he has never missed a date.

My best friend is QUIET,
he speaks in a still, small voice that proves he's near
His arm is not shortened that he cannot save,
nor his ear deaf that he cannot hear.

My best friend is RICH,
he has abundant wealth.
He promises to supply all my needs,
and that includes good health.

My best friend is STRONG,
he tells me to be strong and courageous, too
When worry or fear creeps in,
I stand my ground like I was instructed to do.

My best friend is TALKATIVE,
he always has something to say
We both look forward to our time of prayer
and fellowship, every single day.

My best friend is THOUGHTFUL,
he records every good deed I do
When I give, he will repay me,
and repay all his other friends, too.

My best friend is TRUE,
that's how he wants me to be
True to him, others and myself too,
so the truth will set me free.

My best friend is TRUSTWORTHY,
he encourages me to rely on him.
His promises are genuine,
and I can trust him to keep them.

My best friend is UNDERSTANDING,
I've hurt him many a time
When I admit I'm wrong,
he not only forgives, he forgets my crime.

My best friend is VICTORIOUS,
no enemy great or small has ever defeated him
He fights against those who fight against me,
and gives me victory over them.

My best friend is WISE,
yet he's not puffed up with pride
When making decisions,
I first seek his counsel, then follow his guide.

My best friend is XENIAL,
he welcomes strangers and foreigners in his heart
Anyone who comes into his presence,
he invites them to stay and never depart.

My best friend is YOUTHFUL,
he never grows old and loses touch with reality
From generation to generation,
he exhibits the same vim, vigor and vitality.

My best friend is ZEALOUS, and I'm not jealous,
because his new friends are mine, too
All friends are fruitful branches on his vine,
and there's room enough for you.

Jesus Christ is my best friend.
I thank God for the day we met.
His goodness and mercy assure me,
that I don't know Him well enough yet.

And you are my friends if you do what I command you.
(John 15:14 NASB)

38.

Effie, MY FRIENDSHIP TREE

Dear Effie,

I thank God for you.
You invited me to visit your family church
Knowing the back of a truck was my only ride
You inspired me to join the junior usher board
And I appreciate you for staying by my side.
You introduced me to my first love
During years of country living.
We walked and talked among our favorite pines
and like the cones they produced,
you kept right on giving.
Relationships with the brothers
Challenged both of us you know,
But the pain of marital separation
Turned out for good. It helped us both to grow.
Living face-to-face on the same street,
As single-parent moms taking good care of our kids
We learned how to manage our money well
And never made foolish Bingo bids.
In the name of fun we laughed and had a good time.
It's too bad I slept through
all the preacher's sermons on sin.
Aren't you glad Jesus never gave up on us
When we hung out in places we should not have been?
Sometimes we went our separate ways
But we knew how to work, play and party well.

Jesus was patient with both of us, until He finally said,
"Either come to me or go to hell."
Well, I must confess that I'm older and wiser now,
And after a few close calls with death,
I know Jesus is real. He's still watching us.
He controls every move and every breath.
Girl, thank you for being my life-long friend,
You have been there through thick and thin.
Looking back over my life, I think about you
And pray that our friendship will never end.

A friend loves at all times,
and a brother is born for adversity.
(Proverb 17:17 NASB)

39.

The SUN and The SON

Does anyone understand the sun?
It always rises in the east and sets in the west,
right on time, day after day.

On cloudy days its rays still shine through
to remind us of its presence,
for nothing can hide its light.

The sun lights up the entire world around us,
just as Jesus lights up the world inside of us.

We're happy when the sun's warmth is felt
and its beauty seen,
but sad when the weather is dark and dreary.
Sunlight is not seen at night,
for darkness has no fellowship with light.

When the sun shines, the whole creation is revealed.
When darkness comes, the whole creation is concealed.

Sunlight is provided for both the saved
and lost sinners alike.
Some walk in the light
while others cherish the night.

No computer operates the sun,
for it is high above the earth and reigns over it.

Can anyone explain the sun?
Can man make it reverse its course
and rise in the west instead of in the east?
What is its energy source? Where does it get its light?

How can this big shiny ball above our city be seen in distant
places at the same time?
Does the sun follow us wherever we go?
Or is it already there to greet us when we arrive?

Why do we encounter both light and darkness
every single day?
Could this be a fresh reminder
to choose daily between life and death?

Sunlight trickles through when we choose
sheer window coverings.
But its full warmth and light are not experienced
until we open wide or remove all barriers.

When we shut out the light,
darkness comes and we see nothing,
When light comes, immediately
it drives out all darkness.

Just as the SUN rises each new day
and invites us to come and walk in its light;
Jesus, the SON of God,
invites us to open up our hearts and let him,
the light of the world, come in.

When we reject the S-U-N sun, we walk in darkness.
When we reject the S-O-N son, we are eternally lost.

40.

That's Winter To Me

When autumn leaves on tree branches disappear
And chilly winds spoil outdoor fun
The warmth of a fireplace beckons me to draw near
That's winter to me.

When snowflakes blanket streets with a hush,
And snowplows, cars, shovels and rubber soles
Leave tracks and generate dirty slush
That's winter to me.

When mercury drops bitter cold penetrates my bones
And I act to prevent colds, flu, and frozen water pipes,
My delight is in hot tea rather than ice cream cones
That's winter to me.

When heavy coats, boots, gloves, scarves, hats,
Earmuffs, knits, mitts, sweaters, and wool gear
Make me feel like I'm hauling a bundle of baseball bats
That's winter to me.

When smoke oozes from my nose and mouth
Crisp air makes lips chap, teeth rattle, fingertips numb,
Desire for warmer weather make me head south
That's winter to me.

When days are short and nights too long
And Christmas celebrations have waxed and waned,
My prayers for spring to hurry up don't seem wrong
That's winter to me.

41.

Christmas Time

'Tis time to unwind as Christmas Day draws nigh
'Tis time to kiss wisdom in finance goodbye
'Tis time for purses and wallets to sigh
'Tis time to understand the reason why...
'Twas Christmas Eve when expectancy ran high
'Twas Christmas Day when the world received God's gift
of love named Jesus,
a priceless treasure that money cannot buy.

MERRY CHRISTMAS!

42.

Why Don't We Trust In The Lord?

We trust in the preacher to tell us God's word
We trust the lawyer to get our case heard
We trust in a key to start the car's motor
We trust air freshener to eliminate a foul odor.
But why don't we trust in Jesus?

We trust a cute doll to make a little girl smile
We trust in a friend to go that extra mile
We trust the doctor knows when he says, "It's a boy!"
We trust that a bicycle will make a delightful toy.
But why can't we trust in the Lord?

We trust the teacher to tell us what's right
We trust the power company to provide us with light
We trust in our parents to feed and clothe us
We trust an appetizing meal to satisfy our stomachs.
But somebody tell me, why don't we trust in Jesus?

We believe that a key will unlock the door
We believe a man's asleep when we hear him snore
We believe fried chicken is finger lickin' good
We believe that beneath a tree's bark there is wood.
So, why can't we believe in Jesus?

We obey the red traffic light that tells us to stop
We obey the signal when flagged by a cop

We obey parents and drink the cold remedy
of hot lemon tea and honey
We obey the government and pay our tax money.
But why won't we obey Jesus?

We trust a chair to support our weight
We trust a boyfriend to show up for a date
We trust the postal service and Internet to deliver
Christmas cards
We trust the quarterback to gain extra yards.
But why don't we trust in Jesus?

We tell our children about Santa Claus,
The Easter Bunny, the Tooth fairy, and the Boogey Man
But do we tell them the story of Jesus?

We say to each other, "I love you."
We sometimes say, "I hate you!"
We fuss and we fight,
and call ourselves making up that night.
But do we ever say, "Lord, I love you"?

We hurt other people with evil words and deeds
We justify our behavior to satisfy our own needs.
But do we think to ask, "Lord, help me please?"

My friends, if you believe there's a need
every day of the year
To remember Jesus Christ,
the Savior Christians hold dear
Raise your hands in praise
and recite the following lines
With a heart full of love and Christ on your minds:

I believe in the Father, the Creator of heaven and earth.
I believe in Jesus, God's only begotten Son,
and rejoice at his birth.
I will trust in the Lord with all my heart
I will let the joy of the Lord command doubt to depart
I will obey God's word and follow Christ's example
I will let my own Christian witness be a worthy sample.
God can trust me to help fulfill his plan
to spread the good news
to every boy, girl, woman and man.

43.

Jesus Christ Is Lord

Mary was just a young girl
A virgin like her mother used to be
When an angel said, "You're going to have a baby,"
And Mary asked, "How can this be?"

"Now don't be afraid, Mary,"
Gabriel gently said,
"God is very pleased with you,
His chosen maiden from among a few.

"The Holy Spirit will come upon you
And God's power will rest on you too,
Give birth to a son and name him Jesus
That's all you have to do.

"The holy child will be a great king
And save his people from all their sin.
As Son of the Most High God
His kingdom will have no end."

They **knew that Jesus**, Jesus Christ is Lord
This Jesus Christ is Lord.

"I am the servant of the Lord," said Mary,
"And I believe your message is true.
I know for my own self
There's nothing my God cannot do."

Now Mary was engaged to Joseph
A righteous and just man,
When he found out about her pregnancy
He started to make a new plan.

But an angel appeared to Joseph,
In a dream that changed his life.
So Joseph swallowed his pride
And took pregnant Mary to be his wife.

Joseph and Mary went to Bethlehem
The place where Jesus was born
The babe they wrapped in swaddling cloths
And laid in a manger on Christmas morn.

They knew that Jesus, Jesus Christ is Lord
This Jesus Christ is Lord.

An angel told some shepherds
"I have good news for you.
This day your Savior is born
and the cloths and manger will prove it to you. "

The shepherds heard angels singing
The heavenly host appeared everywhere.
Eager to see the babe in Bethlehem
They hurried off to get there.

They found the parents, and Christ child too
And proof of every word
With joy they returned to their flocks
Praising God for all they'd seen and heard.

They knew that Jesus, Jesus Christ is Lord
This Jesus Christ is Lord.

Some wise men came from the east
To worship the babe born in the hay
A bright star led them all the way
And stopped o'er the place where Jesus lay.

Gifts of gold, frankincense, and myrrh
The wise men presented to him.
They humbly bowed before the brand new king
Who had come into the world to save them.

They knew that Jesus, Jesus Christ is Lord
This Jesus Christ is Lord.

The King of kings and Lord of lords
Is Jesus who bled and died on the cross.
Jesus says, "I am the way, the truth, and the life,"
Don't let the devil be your boss.

Jesus Christ is Lord!
These words one day, everybody will say.
Praise God for his gift to us
Over two thousand years ago one blessed day.

I know that Jesus, Jesus Christ is Lord.
This Jesus Christ is Lord.

Do you know that Jesus, Jesus Christ is Lord?
Then let me hear you say,
"Thank you for saving me Jesus,

I give myself to you.
Body, soul, and spirit
Now give me all of you too."
I know that Jesus, Jesus Christ is Lord!
This Jesus Christ is Lord.

Say it once for the Father now,
"Jesus, Jesus Christ is Lord."
Again for the Son now,
"Jesus, Jesus Christ is Lord."
Once more for the Holy Ghost,
"Jesus, Jesus Christ is Lord. AMEN!"

44.

There's A Time, I Say

Jesus loves you! I declare today
He's the one who washed our sins away.
God sets the time for everything
And this message from Him to you I bring.

Chorus:
There's a time, There's a time, I say, There's a time
There's a time, There's a time, I say, There's a time.

There's a time to laugh and a time to cry
A time to be born and a time to die
There's a time to sow and a time to reap
A time to stay awake, and a time to sleep

There's a time to be hurt and a time to heal
A time for junk food, and a time for a meal
There's a time to mend and a time to tear apart
A time to invite Jesus into your heart

There's a time for sorrow and a time for joy
A time to share the gospel, with every girl and boy
There's a time to mourn and a time to dance
A time to hold position, and a time to advance

There's a time to love and a time to hate
A time to hurry up and a time to wait

There's a time to embrace and a time to refrain
A time for sunshine and a time for rain

There's a time to find and a time to lose
A time to accept and a time to refuse
There's a time to save, and a time to throw away
A time to sing and a time to pray

There's a time to run and a time to walk
A time to be silent and a time to talk
There's a time to teach and a time to test
A time to be active and a time to rest

There's a time to come together and a time to part
A time to love people with all of your heart
There's a time to rise and a time to descend
A time to praise the Lord and shout "Amen!"

There's a time to work and a time to play
A time called night and a time called day.
There's a time to kill and a time to let live
A time for confession and a time to forgive

There's a time to be young and a time to be old
A time to be shy and a time to be bold
There's a time to choose heaven or a place called hell
A time to hear the truth, and understand it well

There's a time for war and a time for peace
A time to hold on and a time to release
There's a time to give and a time to receive
A time to determine just what you believe

And so my friends before it's too late
I urge you to set your priorities straight
The time is now! Don't procrastinate.
Now is the time for decision, do not hesitate.

There's a time, there's a time, I say, there's a time.
Now is the time, now is the time, I say, now is the time.

45.

Graduation Day

To the tune of "Pomp and Circumstance"
The colorful procession begins.
Caps, gowns, collars, and keepsake tassels
Cumulative units or credit hassles
Remind us of how formal education ends.

The infamous struggle to make the grade
Has become a dream of years gone by.
Concentration on beginning your career
Is important for reasons not yet quite clear.
Finally, your name is called. "At last!" you sigh.

No longer a candidate for graduation;
your day has come.
Following participation in commencement
exercises endured,
You cross the stage to claim that precious
piece of paper
That indicates the conclusion of society's
academic caper.
The passport to higher education and work
you just secured.

CONGRATULATIONS!

46.

My Healing Prayer

Dear Lord, I thank you for healing my body, mind, and
emotions. With complete confidence in your Word,
I command every organ and system, every tissue and cell,
every muscle, ligament, bone, joint, and gland in my body
to function in the perfection to which they were designed.
Show me your power to restore my health.

I am fearfully and wonderfully made in your image
and that my soul knows quite well. I request a healing
miracle because you said to ask and I shall receive.
I am a believer and not a doubter. I believe in miracles.
So do again in our times the great and mighty miracles
that you worked in Bible times.

You promised not to withhold any good thing
from those who put their trust in you.
Give me favor with everyone responsible
for my physical and mental wellbeing.
I bind up worry, fear, anxiety and depression
associated with medical reports.
By Jesus' stripes, I am healed.
Thank you for working through doctors and medicine.

You will keep me in perfect peace
because my mind is stayed on you and I trust you.
I pray a hedge of protection around myself.

No weapon formed against me shall prosper.
The blood of Jesus flows through my veins
and washes out all harmful bacteria and diseased germs
from the crown of my head to the soles of my feet.

Nothing shall steal my joy
because the joy of the Lord is my strength.
Bless me to be strong in faith and to remember
that greater is He that is in me than he that is in the world.
I am more than a conqueror through Jesus Christ who loves
me. Thank you for a powerful healing testimony to share
with others.

I shall not die, but live and declare the works of the Lord.
I am healed. I speak it even before I see
the manifestation of answered prayers.
Lord, you said, "Call to me and I will answer you
and show you great and mighty things that you know not."
Therefore I pray and anticipate positive results in Jesus'
name. Amen.

*"Being cheerful keeps you healthy. It is slow death to be gloomy
all the time."*

(Proverbs 17:22 GNT)

47.

Preschool Teacher

Teacher, Teacher, I know my ABC's.
Teacher, Teacher, What is this? What are these?
Teacher, Teacher, I bumped my knee.
Teacher, Teacher, Help me make a "T."
Teacher, Teacher, Let me help you.
Teacher, Teacher, Show me what to do.
Teacher, Teacher, I've got a nasty nose.
Teacher, Teacher, She stepped on my toes.
Teacher, Teacher, That boy hit me.
Teacher, Teacher, How big am I going to be?
Teacher, Teacher, Is it time to go home yet?
Teacher, Teacher, I got a puppy. He's my pet.
Teacher, Teacher, I put my book high on the shelf.
Teacher, Teacher, I spilled milk on myself.
Teacher, Teacher, She took my seat.
Teacher, Teacher, I'm hungry. I want to eat.
Teacher, Teacher, I can't see. That boy is in my way.
Teacher, Teacher, I'm not sleepy. I took a nap yesterday.
Teacher, Teacher, Oh, I forgot your name.
You're nice like my mommy and I love you the same.

48.

Goodbye Depression

Depression knocked on my door
And my lonely self invited her in.
I embraced her with a smile,
Delighted to have companionship awhile.

She sat a moment and sighed,
Then forgot her manners and invaded my space.
It felt nice when she snuggled close to me
So I relaxed and made us hot tea.

It was the joyous Christmas season
When I welcomed my guest who made herself comfortable.
She ruined all desire for festivities, delicacies, and music galore,
And stayed so long 'til I didn't like company anymore.

Depression strolled from room to room.
She took over like she owned my humble abode.
Helpless, I gave in until a voice from deep within
Whispered, "I love you. I am with you my friend."

"Call to me and I will answer you, and show you
Great and mighty things you do not know."
Energy zapped and mind confused,
I cried, "Help me God! I'm being abused!"

A supernatural power seized control of me
And words exploded out of my mouth.
"Get out Depression!
The God of love has heard my cry."
Instantly, she loosed her grip and fled
Amid my hearty, "Goodbye!"

He gives power to the weak and strength to the powerless.
(Isaiah 40:29 NLT)

49.

Aging Gracefully

Don't let the excitement of youth cause you to forget your Creator. Honor him in your youth before you grow old and say, "Life is not pleasant anymore."

(Ecclesiastes 12:1 You Version)

On October 22, 2016, I stood among a crowd of people staring at the sunny sky as a bunch of balloons became airborne at the Grand Opening of radio station KTYMgospel.net in Inglewood, CA. Suddenly, a thousand tiny black flying insects attacked my eyes and lightning flashed in my eyes. Without warning, my vision was under attack! I swatted at the swarming horde of critters before my eyes. They kept on coming and lightning kept on flashing. I noticed that I, alone, was swinging at them. What was I to do?

I headed to Urgent Care for a chat with a physician.
"Do you see lines, dots, insects, or bigger animals?"
"They look like a bunch of black gnats," I said.
"You mean you've heard of this happening before?"
"Sure. They are called floaters. They come with age. Sometimes they go away. Sometimes more come later. Your eyes will adjust to them. Just come back if the critters get bigger."

I went home and told some senior friends about the attack on my eyes.

"Oh, you're talking about floaters," one said.

"I've had them for years."

"Really! I never heard of such a thing," I said.

"I hadn't either until the day I was riding in the passenger seat and started swatting at flies," she said. "My husband was driving."

"What are you doing?" he said.

"Don't you see those flies in here?" I said.

"What flies?"

"The flies that keep flying in my face."

"There are no flies in here," he said.

Another friend said, "Oh, floaters!"

She laughed and said, "A man came to my house wearing a white shirt. While he sat talking to me, I saw ants crawling on his long sleeve. I was tempted to brush them off but then they would get inside my house. So I just watched them crawl on him. That's how I discovered floaters."

A third woman said, "I kept picking at a black speck in my drink and I could never get it out. That's when I knew something was wrong."

As I listened to them, I realized that I'd never heard any lessons on what to expect on my senior trip. So I decided to share some observations from a senior perspective to encourage younger people to appreciate their youthfulness and to give some insights regarding frequent concerns I discovered (with the help of others, of course) about this aging process.

77 Quick Tips for the Senior Trip

	Frequent Concerns	Frequent Fixes Applied
1.	Constipation/ bowel irregularity	Prunes and prune juice/Metamucil
2.	Dehydration	Drink lots of water
3.	Joint stiffness, aches and pains	Keep on moving. Walk it out!
4.	Moles and age spots	Wide-brimmed hat/sunscreen/shades
5.	Starches turning into sugar	Drink Cranberry juice
6.	High blood pressure	Garlic and apple cider vinegar
7.	Fear of falling	Wear flats, use a cane or walker
8.	Overwhelmed by Doctor appointments	Keep a calendar and update it
9.	Hair turns gray/thins/ disappears	Flaunt it! Dye it/wear a wig or hat
10.	Don't feel like cooking	Meals on Wheels/eat out/phone in
11.	Concerns about your wealth	Donate to charity/splurge on self
12.	Dry, cracked feet, corns, callouses	See a podiatrist/drink more water
13.	Forgetting to take medicines	Fill a Sunday-Saturday pillbox
14.	Poking along on the freeway	Drive the streets/call for a ride
15.	Fear of heart attack and stroke	Take a baby aspirin daily
16.	Insomnia	Stop worrying before going to bed
17.	Slower thinking/ memory failing	Crossword puzzles/read books
18.	Edema/water retention	Limit salt intake/Move around
19.	Impotence and desire is gone	Testosterone shots/ Viagra
20.	Vaginal dryness	Use vaginal lubricants
21.	Need help around the house	Hire a handyman/ housekeeper
22.	Imbalance and coordination	Line dance/keep the body moving

23.	Feeling depressed/down	Help someone/call prayer partner
24.	Want to stay informed	Join AARP (they know everybody)
25.	Can't get to the bank	Enroll in direct deposit
26.	Fewer friends	Make new friends on Facebook
27.	Bored/Desire to talk to someone	Become a church/ Walmart greeter
28.	Not enough life insurance	Save extra money each month
29.	Feeling useless	Volunteer
30.	Excess fat around the midsection	Exercise/fruits and vegetables
31.	Shoulders stoop/posture changes	Physical therapy/ chiropractor
32.	Forgetting bill due dates	Sign up for automatic/bill pay
33.	Medical directive & power of attorney	Fill out papers. Just do it!
34.	No longer driving	Access a ride/Uber/Lyft/ friend
35.	Afraid retirement means death	Retire! Think positive thoughts
36.	Grown children won't leave home	Move into senior housing
37.	Fear of side effects to meds	Flush meds with lots of water
38.	Osteoporosis	Calcium along with vitamin D3
39.	Calls from IRS /telemarketers	Let voicemail answer for you
40.	Urinary incontinence	Wear Depends
41.	Fallen arches (feet spread out)	Wear wider, bigger shoes
42.	Wrinkles and sagging skin	Facials/upward strokes only
43.	Slowed and limited movement	Keep on moving! Start early.
44.	Fear of signing the wrong documents	Pray and trust God
45.	Acid reflux	No dairy/Take Antacids-Tums

46.	Fear of nursing home placement	Keep moving to stay fit/pray
47.	Impaired vision	Bifocals/trifocals/magnifying glass
48.	Increased flatulence	Beware of cabbage, beans, broccoli
49.	Technologically-challenged	Take classes (FREE from Apple)
50.	Cataracts/glaucoma	Get regular visual exams
51.	Bones break easily/heal slowly	Vitamin D-egg yolks/salmon/tuna
52.	Circulation problems/ numbness	Yoga/exercise/leg massages
53.	Energy declines/tire easily	Eat more greens, less meat
54.	Body temperature changes	Get a throw/keep a wrap
55.	Menopausal hot flashes/night sweats	Meditation/acupuncture may help
56.	Trouble getting out of a chair	Rock back and forth (1-2-3- lift off)
57.	Risk of infection and inflammation	Lose excess weight/exercise
58.	Fewer teeth/ dentures	Dentures/partial/ and Fixodent
59.	Height decreases as bones in spine thin	Adjust to new height. Stand tall!
60.	Weight loss due to lost muscle tissue	Physical therapy/massage therapy
61.	Fear of being forgotten	Become an organ donor
62.	Imbalance/clumsy/shaky hands	Vitamin B12/no caffeine or alcohol
63.	Hearing loss	Hearing aids
64.	Feeling alone	Believe Jesus is with you always
65.	Feeling old	Rejoice! Enjoy listening to oldies
66.	Less blood volume	Drink more water
67.	Having to use bathroom during the night	Rejoice in being able to get up
68.	Challenged with land & flip phone	Get a Smartphone and apps

69.	Need to go to ER (emergency)	Call paramedics to take you
70.	Fear of Safety	Grip handrails/get rugs that grip
71.	Fear of dying	Make your own final preparations
72.	Fear of probate process	Get a living trust
73.	Feeling lonely	Join a senior group and church
74.	Fear of your final destination	Ask Jesus to save you/ receive Him
75.	Anxious about finishing an assignment	Relax/ be pro-active/ Just do it!
76.	Feeling irritable and angry about aging	Watch comedies and laugh/pray
77.	Fear of last wishes being ignored	Stop it! It won't matter to you!

Bon Voyage!

Meditations for Frequent Concerns of Seniors

1. Fears

"Do not fear, for I am with you; do not anxiously look about you, for I am your God. I will strengthen you, surely I will help you, surely I will uphold you with My righteous right hand."

Isaiah 41:10 NASB

2. Family

Remember God "the Father, from whom every family in heaven and on earth receives its true name."

Ephesians 3:15 GNT

For you are all children of God through faith in Christ Jesus.

Galatians 3:26 NLT

3. Friends

A man who has friends must himself be friendly, but there is a friend who sticks closer than a brother.

Proverbs 18:24 NKJV

4. Finances

And my God shall supply all your need according to his riches in glory by Christ Jesus.

Philippians 4:19 NKJV

5. Feelings

Don't worry about anything; instead, pray about everything.
Tell God what you need, and thank him for all he has done.
Then you will experience God's peace, which exceeds anything
we can understand. His peace will guard your hearts and minds
as you live in Christ Jesus.

Philippians 4:6,7 NLT

6. Faith

Now faith is the substance of things hoped for, the evidence
of things not seen.

Hebrews 11:1 KJV

But without faith it is impossible to please Him, for he who
comes to God must believe that He is, and that He is a
rewarder of those who diligently seek Him.

Hebrews 11:1,6 NKJV

7. Freedom

Freedom is what we have—Christ has set us free! Stand,
then, as free people, and do not allow yourselves to become
slaves again.

Galatians 5:1 GNT

Therefore if the Son makes you free, you shall be free indeed.

John 8:36 NKJV

Be prepared. You're up against far more than you can
handle on your own. Take all the help you can get, every
weapon God has issued, so that when it's all over but the
shouting you'll still be on your feet.

Ephesians 6:13 MSG

And now, dear brothers and sisters, one final thing. Fix your thoughts on what is true, and honorable, and right, and pure, and lovely, and admirable. Think about things that are excellent and worthy of praise.

Philippians 4:8 NLT

50.

Do you Love Me?

Jesus speaks these words to his children and to every person who wants to become one of his children:

I SEE how you carefully choose gifts for special people with the money I blessed you with.
Do you love them more than me?
I HEAR the wonderful words you speak about the woman I chose to be your wife.
Do you love her more than me?
I FEEL your desire for intimacy with the man I sent into your life. Do you love him more than me?
I TASTE the delicious meals you prepare to please the family I gave you.
Do you love your family more than me?
I SMELL the attractive fragrance you smear on that beautiful body I created.
Do you love yourself more than me?
I BELIEVE the skills I've given you are important.
Do you love your work more than me?

My child, I want to know today,
"Do you really love me?"
Perhaps you are not sure. Think about your answer as I explain the meaning of love to you. When I'm through, I will again ask the question,
"Do you love me?"

I. **What is LOVE?**

There are several types of love and I've ranked them from the least to the greatest love.

1. Eros love is the affection between a man and woman. This love is based on physical attraction.

2. Philia love is the affection of a man for a friend. The friend may even be his dog, although I want you to know that I, not a dog, am man's best friend.

3. Storge love is family affection. There is, and rightfully should be, a bond among family members. It was I who established marriage and the family as a divine institution. Families share joy, pain, and sorrow beyond anyone's understanding.

4. Philadelphia love is brotherly love shared between sisters and brothers. This unity is found in my churches where members call each other brother and sister. Let me remind you that true brothers and sisters bear one another's burdens. When one hurts, all hurt. When one rejoices, all rejoice.

5. Philanthropia love is the kindness and courtesy shown toward humanity. When you feed the hungry, give a gift to a beggar, donate clothing to the homeless, visit the sick and those in prison, and open your home to strangers, you show love for humanity.

6. Agape love is my kind of love. It is based on the will and not the emotions. It is the love I showed to you when I was willing to lay down my life to pay for the sins that you committed. I came into the world to

die in your place that you might have the right to
receive eternal life. I willingly obeyed my Father as I
sought to do His will and not my own. I assure you
the greatest love a person can have for his friends is
to give his life for them. Now, haven't I shown my
love for you?

Again, I ask, "Do you love me?"

In I Corinthians chapter thirteen verses four through
eight of the book I inspired men to write, the one you call
the Bible, I clearly defined love. Have you read it?
Listen to my definition of love:

*Love is patient and kind; it is not jealous or conceited or proud;
love is not ill-mannered or selfish or irritable; love does not keep a
record of wrongs; love is not happy with evil, but is happy with the
truth. Love never gives up; and its faith, hope, and patience never fail.
Love is eternal.*

II. How Do You Show Your Love?

I've heard you asking,
"How can I show Jesus my love for him?"
Here's my answer:

If you love me, you will obey my commandments
(John 14:15 GNT).

I've already explained the kind of love you should have.
Now let me explain the word OBEY. Obey means to
listen to and to submit to one's authority. In other
words, it means to comply with or to follow the
directions of another. Your sports authority, Nike, says,

"JUST DO IT!" They both adequately describe what I mean in James chapter one verse twenty-two where I tell you to be doers of the Word and not hearers only.

Whoever accepts my commandments and obeys them is the one who loves me. My Father will love whoever loves me; I too will love him and reveal myself to him. Hear me my child. Whoever loves me will obey my teaching. If you obey my commands, you will remain in my love, just as I obey my Father's commands and remain in his love. My commandment is this: love one another, because love comes from God. Whoever loves is a child of God and knows God. Whoever does not love does not know God, for God is love. And God showed his love for you by sending me, his only Son, into the world, so that you might have life through me. This is what love is: it is not that you have loved God, but that he loved you and sent his Son to be the means by which your sins are forgiven.

My children, if this is how God loves you, then you should love one another. No one has ever seen God, but if you love one another, God lives in union with you, and his love is made perfect in you. Remember, perfect love drives out all fear. You love because God first loved you. If someone says he loves God, but hates his brother, he is a liar. For he cannot love God, whom he has not seen, if he does not love his brother, whom he has seen. I cannot overemphasize my command: whoever loves God must love his brother also. You are my friends if you obey my commands.

Do you love me? If you love me, you will obey my commands. I've chosen the word obey because it is easy to remember. To show your love for me, simply:

Obey my commands; put my Words into practice.

Be faithful unto death.

Endure suffering; if you suffer with me you shall
    reign with me.

Yield not to temptation. Instead, yearn for my
    affection.

You must be under obligation to no one. The only obligation you have is to love one another. Whoever does this has obeyed the Law.

III. What are the benefits for those who love me?

1. I have told you this so that my joy may be in you and that your joy may be complete. The joy of the Lord is your strength.

2. My peace, which is far beyond human understanding, will keep your heart and mind safe in union with me.

3. I will fight against those who fight against you and oppose those who oppose you.

4. Your steps will be ordered in my Word. Remember me in all that you do and I will show you the right way.

5. No weapon formed against you shall prosper, and you will have an answer for all who accuse you.

6. Whatever you ask in my name I will give it to you. Delight yourself in me and I shall give you the desires of your heart.

7. What no one ever saw or heard, what no one ever thought could happen, is the very thing I have prepared for those who love me.

IV. How do you show obedience to me?

In conclusion, my child, my children, let me remind you that I am coming back soon. There are a few last things I encourage you to do in order to show your obedience until I return:

1. Spend time alone with me just as you enjoy doing with your human lovers. I will give up whole nations to save your life because you are precious to me and because I love you and give you honor. **Worship me alone.**

2. Let the world know I am yours and you are mine. Tell it wherever you go. If you are ashamed of me and of my teaching in this godless and wicked day, then I will be ashamed of you when I come in the glory of my Father with the holy angels. **Witness to others.**

3. Be faithful until I come. Give thanks always, pray without ceasing, praise me for the blessings of each new day, trust me to keep my promises (I will do it), and serve me with gladness. **Wait on Me.**

Do you love me?

If your answer is "Yes" then you can be certain that nothing can separate you from my love: neither death nor life, neither angels nor other heavenly rulers or powers, neither the present nor the future, neither the world above nor the world below—there is nothing in all creation that will ever be able to separate you from the love of God which is yours through Christ Jesus your Lord.

During the last days there will be such a spread of evil that many people's love will grow cold. But whoever holds out to the end will be saved. To those who win the victory I will give the right to sit beside me on my throne, just as I have been victorious and now sit by my Father on his throne.

If you have ears, then, hear my words and obey.
Have you heard me?
Once more I ask you, "Do you love me?"

Scripture References

John 14:15
James 1:22
1 Corinthians 13:4-8
1 John 4:7-12
Philippians 4:6
Psalm 35:1
Proverb 3:6
John 14:14
Mark 8:38
Revelation 22:12
Psalm 100:2
2 Corinthians 2:9
Revelation 3:21, 22
John 21:15-17

John 14:21, 23
John 15:10, 12
Romans 8:17
1 John 4:18-21
John 15:11, 13
Psalm 37:4
Isaiah 54:17
Romans 13:8
Isaiah 43:4
Galatians 6:2
Romans 8:38,39
Matthew 24:12, 13
Ephesians 6:17
Hebrews 10:23
and others

51.

Spunky

Spunky, an old fellow who loved to eat,
Took one bite of barbecued meat.
With a painful shout,
His false teeth fell out,
So he gummed his delicious treat.

Spunky, an energetic preacher in LA,
an energetic man who could really pray,
Once hollered too loud,
and scared the crowd,
So, he muzzles his mouth to this day.

Spunky, a hothead in Idaho, age forty-five,
Wanted to experience a nosedive.
His wife thought him insane,
When they boarded a plane.
He bailed out, but she did not survive.

Spunky, a man with a tongue sharp as a sickle,
Lacked compassion for the meek and fickle.
A strong east wind came by
and scooped him up to the sky.
Oh, how this mighty man found himself in a pickle!

There once was a proud, skinny dancer named Spunky,
a hip-hop and gospel music junkie.
He slipped on a banana peel
and considered it no big deal,
Till a broken tailbone made him wish he was chunky.

Spunky, a confused journalist in Los Angeles read:
I've never seen the righteous forsaken, nor his seed
begging bread.
"If the homeless are all sinners out on the street,
Begging for change and something to eat,
Why do they say, "God bless you"? he said.

Spunky, a foolish fellow, seduced by swaying hips,
Enticing words, painted eyelids, and luscious lips,
Followed a woman to his doom.
Alas! Her husband entered the room
While he zipped, she nibbled on chips.

Spunky, a robust guy, hired a girl for pleasure galore.
He reserved Room 44, expecting fun beyond the door.
He followed her like an ox to the slaughter,
A chick young enough to be his daughter,
'Til she flashed her badge and hurled him to the floor.

Spunky, a responsible youth with an absentee dad,
Prepared Mom's birthday dinner to make her glad.
The family cat seized his fried fish
and left behind an empty dish.
"I'm going to kill that cat!" he cried, quite mad.

Spunky suffers from arrogance and pride.
He gets upset when people deride him and his bride.
He ignores reproof and goes astray
And encourages others to live his way.
When roasted or fried, loyal followers with him abide.

Spunky preaches powerful messages for everyone.
His lessons come from God who gave us Jesus, His Son.
Like poignant arrows, his words do pierce.
They instruct the gentle and the fierce;
Truth penetrates like bullets from a smoking gun.

There was a homeless veteran named Spunky
Who lived on a sidewalk that smelled funky.
A youth assumed Spunky lacked self-worth
And asked, "Why are you on this earth?"
"To defend my country so YOU won't be a flunky."

Spunky, a fellow who liked to share food for thought
to his friends, a challenging question brought:
"The fool says in his heart there is no God,
But our heart often softens before the final nod.
So is it ever too late to believe as Jesus says we ought?"

Spunky, a betting man who played the slots,
Knew exactly when to shake the spots
Till a maiden who displayed care,
Enticed him and made a dare.
He exchanged his winning knack for the hots.

Spunky, a jolly fella, lived near a river,
Neighbors nicknamed him "the giver."
"I don't need veggies," he did say.
But in his backyard he did stay
Till homemade moonshine destroyed his liver.

Spunky hid in the shadows to avoid disgrace
But once in a while he showed his face.
Acne here and warts there,
He expected people to stare,
When all that mattered was his money in every place.

Spunky, who says, "Surely your sins will find you out."
Observed brawling neighbors and this did shout:
"Tis better to remain silent, than be belligerent!
Let people think you're ignorant
Rather than open your mouth and remove all doubt!"

Spunky practices sermons on his Husky named Pearl
Her feedback is valued more than anyone in the world
When bored she groans and pouts
When excited she jumps and shouts
The message is just right, when he sees her tail curl.

Spunky, the husband of a nagging wife,
Made plans to end his constant strife.
He put a bed on the roof
that suddenly went "POOF!"
When she poked his inflatable bed with a knife.

52.

We'll See You Later

My Dear Friend,
We regret that you had to leave us so soon.
It's too bad that many, you never got a chance to know,
Even though your ministry helped them to grow.
We'll see you later.

Servant of God, your suffering put our faith to the test.
Your gifts and talents you used to the very end.
Your sacrificial commitment is hard to comprehend.
We'll see you later.

It's hard to say goodbye when you left so much undone
While we try to imagine a place without tears or pains,
You're reaping rewards in heaven where God reigns.
We'll see you later.

"Do not be worried and upset," Jesus told them. "Believe in God and believe also in me. There are many rooms in my Father's house, and I am going to prepare a place for you. I would not tell you this if it were not so. And after I go and prepare a place for you, I will come back and take you to myself, so that you will be where I am."
John 14:1-3 GNT